# Baptist Distinctives

# Baptist Distinctives

## A Pattern for Service

by

**R. Dowd Davis**

STEVENS BOOK PRESS
Wake Forest, North Carolina

BAPTIST DISTINCTIVES:
A Pattern for Service

All Scripture quotations are from the Revised Standard Version
of the Bible, copyright 1946, 1952, and © 1971, 1973 by the
Division of Christian Education, National Council of
Churches in Christ.

Copyright © 1986 by R. Dowd Davis
*All rights reserved*

ISBN 0-913029-11-4

**Library of Congress Cataloging-in-Publication Data**

Davis, R. Dowd.
  Baptist distinctives.

  Bibliography: p.
  1. Baptists — Doctrines. 2. Baptists — Apologetic works. 3. Southern Baptist Convention — Doctrines. 4. Southern Baptist Convention — Apologetic works. I. Title.
BX6331.2.D38   1986         286'.132         86-5802
ISBN 0-913029-11-4 (pbk.)

**STEVENS BOOK PRESS**
**245 E. Roosevelt Ave.**
**P.O. Box 71, Wake Forest, NC 27587**
**Telephone 919-556-3830**

*Printed in the USA*

DEDICATED TO

My Father

MARION LESLIE DAVIS, SR.

devoted servant to

The Beaufort Baptist Church
for fifty years as Clerk,
Deacon and Sunday School
teacher

and to

The Atlantic Baptist Association
for thirty eight years as Moderator

# Table of Contents

|     | Introduction ............................. ix |
| --- | --- |
| 1.  | The Buck Stops Here ..................... 1 |
| 2.  | A Place to Stand ......................... 13 |
| 3.  | We Are a Royal Priesthood................. 23 |
| 4.  | An Essential Difference.................... 35 |
| 5.  | On Getting Down to Brass Tacks ........... 47 |
| 6.  | Conclusions .............................. 57 |
|     | Selected Bibliography .................... 63 |

# Introduction

There is a revolution occurring among Southern Baptists today. The conviction which has motivated us since 1845 is crumbling. Until recently, we have believed we could ignore doctrinal, sociological and political differences among Baptists in different parts of the country in order to pool our resources for missions, education and social ministries. Lately, however, the spirit of mutual trust and cooperation which has motivated our Convention throughout most of her history has been giving way to a spirit of distrust and competition. Basic to this change of motivation is a corresponding alteration in our understanding of what it means to be a Baptist.

It has always been difficult to define precisely what it means to be a Baptist because of the very nature of the ideas which brought us into being. Our forebears emphasized different ideas and practices at different times and different places. From the earliest appearance of Baptists in England in the seventeenth century, we have been a contentious people. At that time differences among the various groups included the mode of baptism, some practicing pouring, (or effusion) and others immersion. In addition, there were important doctrinal differences. The so-called Particular Baptists followed the teaching of John Calvin that only certain "particular" individuals who had been predestined by God would be saved. Logically, of course, this implied that everyone else was predestined to be damned. On the other hand, General Baptists believed in the interpretation of one, Jacob Arminius, who taught that salvation was available "generally" to anyone who would accept Jesus Christ as his Savior.

These differences were brought into the new world by the English Baptists who came to the American colonies largely to escape persecution by the established churches of Europe. In America, Particular Baptists began to be called Regular Baptists and General Baptists, Original Free Will Baptists. Other divisions occurred over the propriety of missions and Christian education, some supporting one or both of these ministries, others opposing one or both. For example, Baptists in North Carolina divided in the early years of the nineteenth century over the question of missions. Those who believed in Predestination looked upon missions and evangelism as not only useless, but as an affront to the sovereignty of God, who had already decided the ones to be saved and those to be damned. These called themselves Primitive Baptists, but were often called "Hardshell" Baptists by those who disagreed with them. Later another rupture occurred when, in 1830, certain Baptists gathered in Greenville, North Carolina to organize a convention for the purpose of supporting Christian education as well as supporting missions more effectively.

More recently, differences have arisen concerning the requirements for participation in the Lord's

## Introduction

Supper. Some churches have invited to the Lord's Table all who profess faith in Jesus Christ as Savior and Lord without regard for baptism or other denominational affiliation. Others have welcomed those who have been immersed in any church, while still others have insisted that immersion be administered by the minister of a properly constituted Baptist church before one is invited to participate. Finally, a few have excluded everyone except the members of the specific Baptist congregation which is celebrating the Supper. These are but a few of the major concerns which have divided Baptists from one another at various times. In addition to these, there have been many lesser causes for disagreement. Therefore, it is often difficult to define precisely what a Baptist believes or does.

But as one reads our history certain themes repeatedly reoccur, and a pattern gradually develops which is consistent in most of those groups who have called themselves Baptists. (Perhaps it would be helpful at this point to note that we who are called Baptists did not originally choose this name for ourselves. Rather, as in the case of the early Christians at Antioch in Syria, the name was applied to us in derision by those who have objected to our insistence upon Believers' Baptism.) These themes, while none may be unique to Baptists in itself, together form a pattern that is unique. We call them Baptist Distinctives, not because they are our sole possession, but because together they have characterized us at most times and places in our history. Admittedly, these distinctives are not central to the proclamation of the Gospel, but they determine in large measure how we live that Gospel day by day. Other Christian groups have devised their own means for putting their convictions into practice; Baptist Distinctives are our particular method of practicing our faith. It is primarily in the differences between these various methods that lie the distinctive qualities of the various Christian denominations and churches.

It is these very Baptist Distinctives which establish our unique identity among Christian groups that are being altered in the revolution threatening our Convention. For it appears obvious to many that if this revolution is consolidated the Southern Baptist Convention will no longer continue to be what she has been for 140 years. Rather, she will be transformed into something else, motivated by a spirit different from that which has characterized her heretofore.

It is out of this concern that the present essay has been written. The various chapters were originally prepared as sermons which were preached to the congregation of the Littleton Baptist Church to acquaint those people with the nature of the conflict as the author sees it. Those sermons have since been edited rather extensively to adapt the peculiarities of the spoken medium to the very different requirements of the written medium. However, the essential concerns and development are the same. The writer is aware that they are in no sense scholarly contributions to the theological world. Rather, they are primarily addressed to those members of Southern Baptist churches who, for whatever reasons, have never enjoyed the privilege of studying at a Southern

Baptist theological seminary. Whatever we may have been throughout our history, Baptists have always been people who were concerned about the thinking and actions of the rank and file in our churches. Thus, it is important for our people to be informed. It is the hope of the present writer that his efforts may contribute to their information.

# 1
# The Buck Stops Here

Everything human has a beginning, faith no less than life itself. So Baptists as a Christian group distinct from other Christian groups began somewhere. Often, it is only as we look back over the path we have traveled that we are able to perceive the decisive events which have determined that path. The story of Nicodemus in the third chapter of the Gospel of John offers an example of the manner in which faith in Jesus Christ as Savior and Lord may begin. It is used here not because one thinks Nicodemus was a Baptist — indeed, there were no Baptists in those days — nor even that he was a Christian, for the record does not state that he followed Jesus' prescription. Rather, it is used because it sounds like the experience of many Baptists, including that of the present writer.

> Now there was a man of the Pharisees, named Nicodemus, a ruler of the Jews. This man came to Jesus by night and said to him, "Rabbi, we know that you are a teacher come from God; for no one can do these signs that you do, unless God is with him." Jesus answered him, "Truly, truly, I say to you, unless one is born anew, he cannot see the kingdom of God." Nicodemus said to him, "How can a man be born when he is old? Can he enter a second time his mother's womb and be born?" Jesus answered, "Truly, truly,

> I say to you, unless one is born of water and the Spirit, he cannot enter the kingdom of God. That which is born of the flesh is flesh, and that which is born of the Spirit is spirit. Do not marvel that I said to you, 'You must be born again.' The wind blows where it wills, and you hear the sound of it, but you do not know whence it comes or whither it goes; so it is with every one who is born of the Spirit." Nicodemus said to him, "How can this be?" Jesus answered him, "Are you a teacher of Israel, and yet you do not understand this? Truly, truly, I say to you, we speak of what we know, and bear witness to what we have seen; but you do not receive our testimony. If I tell you earthly things and you do not believe, how can you believe if I tell you heavenly things? No one has ascended into heaven but he who descended from heaven, the Son of man. And as Moses lifted up the serpent in the wilderness, so must the Son of man be lifted up, that whoever believes in him may have eternal life." (John 3:1-15)

If ever there was a man who "had it made" it was Nicodemus; for he was a Pharisee and a ruler of the Jews. He had had success and recognition in his chosen profession; he had power and influence over his people. In addition, he must have had wealth, for the requirements of Phariseeism were beyond the attainment of persons who found it necessary to work for a living. As a Pharisee he probably spent most of his time in the study of the Jewish scriptures and the commentaries which earlier rabbis had written. He believed that salvation comes from keeping the Law (the Ten Commandments together with all of the interpretations which had been written concerning them throughout the centuries). He believed that if the Law were kept by all Jews for one Sabbath Day, God would redeem the world. He, as one of the chosen few, had every reason to be satisfied with his life.

*The Buck Stops Here*

And yet, Nicodemus was not satisfied with his life, for he went to Jesus. We do not know what prompted this act, we can only speculate. Perhaps he had witnessed one or more of the signs and wonders Jesus had performed; perhaps he had heard Jesus say something which had shaken the very foundation of his life as a man of God. Certainly something crucial had occurred which had prompted Nicodemus to seek Jesus' help.

In essence, Jesus' response to Nicodemus was to call him to a new relationship with God. For Jesus told him he must be born again. Now, this was important because the Jews of the first century believed that by being born into the people of God, Israel, they were automatically a part of God's kingdom. For them salvation was a community affair. They believed that God had chosen their forefather, Abraham, to be the agent of His saving work in the world and that He had promised Abraham his descendents would be blessed thereby. Nicodemus had been operating on the assumption that he had already been born into God's kingdom.

But Jesus told him he must be born again, or "from above" as the text can also be translated. Apparently, to be born as a Jew was not enough; something else was required. The birth which his parents had given him, the circumcision which was the rite of initiation into the nation of Israel, and all his efforts to understand and keep the Law were insufficient. Nicodemus, said Jesus, must make a self-conscious decision to submit himself to God as an individual person, an act quite separate from his physical birth as a Jew.

Secondly, Jesus said he must receive the Holy Spirit into his life. The Jews believed that in order for one to approach God he must go through the mediation of the priesthood. An individual Jew in the first century was required to worship God by making sacrifices on the altar of the Temple in Jerusalem. Since only the priests could enter the Holy Place and make sacrifices on the altar, the individual Jew could only approach God through the ministry of the priest. It is important to note here that at the time of Nicodemus the High Priests were appointed by the Roman Governor of Judea. This fact placed religion under the control of the government.

But Jesus told Nicodemus that he could approach God directly in the Holy Spirit. The Spirit, He said, is independent of human control and acts, like God, on His own volition. By receiving this Spirit into his life Nicodemus would be relating to God directly.

Finally, Jesus said that this opportunity to relate one's self to God is open to everyone. The Jews of that day believed that salvation was their exclusive possession. They were convinced that in order to be related to God a person must become a Jew. But Jesus said "... that whoever believes in him may have eternal life." Anyone, not just a Jew, could relate himself in a saving way to the God of creation who revealed Himself to men in Jesus.

As Nicodemus learned from Jesus, Baptists have usually begun with the conviction that the beginning point of saving faith is the realization that each individual is responsible for his own relationship with God. He must decide for himself what is to be the foundation of his life, the focus around which he

## The Buck Stops Here

lives, the source of strength and wisdom which informs everything he is, thinks, feels or does. This, we have usually believed, is the most important decision a person will ever make, the decision which validates or invalidates all other decisions.

This conviction is a radical departure from the teaching of most religions, for religion in most cultures has been thought to be too precious and fragile to be entrusted to the gross insensitivities and barbarities of common people. Only an authoritarian religion, it is believed, can adequately protect its sacred teachings and rituals from being profaned.

Judaism was certainly an authoritarian religion in the time of Jesus. And the new Church which arose out of the body of Jesus' followers after His resurrection rapidly became authoritarian with the passage of time. Perhaps it was inevitable that any new faith would tend to become pressed into the mold of authoritarianism by the pressures of the world into which the Gospel came.

The world of the first century into which the Church was born was a brutal, merciless society. The Roman Empire had conquered this world and now ruled it under the philosophy that "might makes right." While there were examples of compassion among the individual Roman citizens from time to time, the exercise of government by the Romans was regularly legalistic, merciless and effective. Such attitudes permeated all areas of life under Roman rule.

The Church was subject to persecution from her very beginnings at Pentecost. The Gospel didn't fit into the Roman way of thinking; it was alien to everything that Roman rule represented. But persecution of the Church was begun by the religious leaders of the Jews in Jerusalem. The Sadducees conducted the rituals of Temple worship under Roman rule only so long as peace and tranquility were maintained among the Jewish people. Jesus' condemnation of the perversion of Temple worship was a threat to the Sadducees' income from the sacrificial system. As more Jews became Christians, the Sadducees feared they would lose revenue. Jesus' claim to be King of the Jews was interpreted by many as a threat of revolt against Roman rule. Such a revolt, it was believed, would result in their loss of their privileges no matter who won. Therefore, the Sadducees were determined to stamp out this new Church. Their persecution of Christians continued until the Church had become predominantly Gentile.

During the time of this Jewish persecution, the attitude of the Roman government toward Christians was largely one of benign indifference. As long as they obeyed the law and paid their taxes they were regarded as Jews who were permitted to practice their faith without interference from Roman authorities. But, when the Emperor Nero was looking for a scapegoat on which to blame the fire which laid waste much of the city of Rome in A.D. 64, he found the Christians a convenient target. Later, toward the end of the first century, sacrifice to the Emperor was made a mandatory pledge of allegiance to Roman rule. Because of their refusal to admit that "Caesar is Lord," Christians became outlaws within the Empire, and the Church became the object of systematic

## The Buck Stops Here

persecution by Roman authorities. Many thousands were burned, crucified, fed to wild animals, imprisoned or exiled.

In addition to years of persecution of Christians, the first three centuries of the Church's existence were also periods of religious ferment. The old classical Greek and Roman religions were generally bankrupt, and people were desperately seeking something to take their places. Each nation which Roman armies conquered contributed its own religions to the spiritual melee. In some cases there were striking similarities between the other religions and the Gospel. Persian Mithraism, for example, also taught a god who had been executed and raised from the dead. In other cases attempts were made to alter Gospel teachings to conform it to other religions. Many Christians were tempted by the Gnostic insistence that Jesus was not a man but only an apparition.

When his life is relatively carefree and there are no threats to his being, one can be rather tolerant of the beliefs and behavior of others. But when one's faith is illegal, when government agents are hunting him and his friends to force them to abandon their beliefs or be killed, tolerance of different beliefs and actions of others becomes a luxury which many believe cannot be afforded. In such cases the world is often perceived as being divided into "us" and "them," and the ties which bind one to his friends become essential to survival.

It is no wonder, then, that Christians in the second and third centuries became radically concerned about beliefs and practices. Those who did not affirm the majority position were often viewed with suspicion by the majority and frequently excommunicated from the fellowship. Nor is it difficult to understand why guardians of the faith were believed necessary and were given the authority to decide what is true and what is false. Thus, the creed which had been developed was used as a test of orthodoxy and the priesthood was charged with safeguarding that creed against perversion or attack.

Needless to say, not everyone was willing to submit to such authoritarian developments within the Church. Thousands objected to various aspects of the creed as it was in the process of development through the years. Many councils were held in order to debate the various statements of faith and to hammer out a statement which would be acceptable to the largest number of persons. But when it was finally adopted, opponents within the Church were ruthlessly opposed and expelled.

Perhaps, as we said, it was inevitable that any new faith would tend to become pressed into the mold of authoritarianism by the pressures of the world into which the Gospel came. Perhaps the new Church could survive only through the development of an authoritarian heirarchy and an exclusive creed during the first three hundred years of her existence. In any case, with the establishment of the Christian religion as the official religion of the Roman Empire by the Emperor Constantine in A.D. 330 this trend was solidly grounded; it continued to develop during the so-called "dark ages" when the Church became the primary repository of Western culture.

And yet, throughout the history of the Church there have arisen those groups which have seen the essential individuality of one's relationship with God which is implicit in the Gospel of Jesus. Such persons have seen the radical departure from the primitive Gospel which had occurred through the years. But, in almost every case, the established Roman Church descended with all her considerable power, often through the agency of the state, to eradicate such "heresies." It is quite true that the attempts of some Baptists to identify such groups as the Waldenses and others as early Baptists fail to note other beliefs of these groups which we would not avow. But, at least the idea of the competency of the individual before God has often surfaced among believers throughout the history of the Church.

It is this history of the experience of dissenters with the Roman Church which has convinced most Baptists of the absolute necessity of complete freedom of conscience for the individual. Neither creed nor heirarchy within the Church nor the establishment of any particular religious group by the state may be allowed to create a test of any individual's faith in Jesus Christ.

The earliest European Baptists quickly found themselves subject to persecution by the established Protestant churches in most countries. It was for this reason that many of them emigrated to the New World in search of religious freedom. But they found that even in some English colonies in America it was against the law to be a Baptist. All citizens in those colonies were required to be baptized as infants into the Church of England or other established church and to pay taxes for its support. Baptist meeting houses were locked and Baptist preachers jailed by the authorities in those colonies. However, in spite of such discouragement, the Baptist message took root and spread rapidly. In their desire for religious freedom, many Baptists supported the American revolution, and Baptists were directly responsible for the adoption of the First Amendment of the United States Constitution which guarantees religious liberty to all. Baptists, often from bitter experience, recognized that if any person is to have religious liberty all must enjoy it.

As in all cases of human judgment, there are dangers in the Baptist view of the competency of the individual before God. First of all, it may tend to exalt excessively the individual's view of himself. He may come to feel that his opinion is adequate without any need for education or experience. Believing himself to be equal to all others, he may come to think that he needs no others, that he is a law unto himself.

A second danger of this view is that its adherent may overlook the community aspects of the Christian Gospel. As we shall see below, one cannot follow Jesus very long before observing that He was very concerned about our relationships with other people and that He had very strong views on the necessity of community for the worship and service of God. A misunderstanding of this doctrine may lead to the self-destructive attempt to live the Christian life by one's self.

Finally, the over-emphasis upon individual competency may tend to fragment the Church and to dissipate her witness in the world. Obviously, individual opinion has little effect upon public opinion in our mass society. It is only as individuals band together into large groups and coordinate their efforts that any one person can make an impact on the world. As an individual, a person has little influence upon the community in which he lives. But as a part of his church he has much more impact as his efforts are combined with those of all the other individuals who comprise his congregation. In addition, there are many facets of Christian ministry which cannot be accomplished by individual persons alone. Missions, education, and social services are some examples of types of ministries which require the pooling of resources by many individuals.

Therefore, whenever individual Baptists allow their personal idiosyncracies to overbalance their sense of community, there is danger not only to the mission of the Church but also to the community herself. Whenever individuals begin to think too highly of themselves and their own particular views, the Church suffers.

It appears that overweening self-regard by certain persons is the root of the current difficulties which threaten to disrupt the Southern Baptist Convention. These individuals who do not know Baptist history, who do not understand the importance of Baptist distinctives, have assumed a disproportionate value for their own views as opposed to the views of others and would impose their views upon all who call ourselves Southern Baptists. A system such as ours requires a precarious balance between overweening self-assertion, on the one hand, and a timid surrender to the pretensions of others, on the other, if it is to succeed.

It is said that during the years of his presidency, Harry Truman kept upon his desk a sign which stated, "The buck stops here." It constantly reminded him that he was ultimately responsible for all decisions involving the national government. Baptists believe that in a similar manner final responsibility for the individual's relationship with God rests upon the invididual, alone. There is no one else who can make such a decision for him. This is where we begin.

# 2
# A Place to Stand

Baptists begin with the conviction that it is the responsibility of each person to decide what will be his relationship with God. He must decide whether to spend his life in living for himself alone or in obedient relationship to the Creator and Sustainer of that life. But having decided on the latter course, he is immediately confronted with another decision. Luke records this decision in the encounter of a lawyer with Jesus.

> And behold, a lawyer stood up to put him to the test, saying, "Teacher, what shall I do to inherit eternal life? He said to him, "What is written in the law? How do you read?" And he answered, "You shall love the Lord your God with all your heart, and with all your soul, and with all your strength, and with all your mind; and your neighbor as yourself." And he said to him, "You have answered right; do this, and you will live." (Luke 10:25-28)

Like Nicodemus, the lawyer had been disturbed by something Jesus had said or done. But, whereas Nicodemus had come to learn from Jesus, it appears the lawyer had come to test Him. He was one of the scribes who devoted their lives to the study of the Law of Moses and the commentaries which had been written about it. Apparently, he felt Jesus was departing from the tradition of Jewish faith, and he wanted to test Jesus' orthodoxy. So he asked Him what God requires of His followers. Jesus, as He often did in such circumstances, responded to the lawyer's question by turning it back upon him. The lawyer's reply quoted from Deuteronomy 6:5 and Leviticus 19:18, which together commanded love for God with one's total being and love for one's neighbor as one's self. Jesus commended his answer and exhorted him to follow his own instruction.

In this dialogue, Jesus pointed out to the lawyer that the essence of life is loving God and loving other persons. Moreover, He was implying that the understanding of the Jews which the lawyer represented was a departure from God's intention in giving the Law to them through Moses. For the Jews by this time had decided that eternal life is earned by obeying the Law; they believed that God is served by keeping a set of rules. Indeed, while God's Law had sought to place relationships with persons in the center of life, the Jewish interpretation of that Law had displaced personal relationships with rules as the center of life. Rules had, in effect, become more important to them than God or other people. On the other hand, Jesus had been saying that God was more concerned with the Jews' relationships with Him and with other people than with their keeping the rules. Jesus was seeking to call the Jews back to God's original purpose for the Law as a guide to help them in their relationships with their Lord and with other persons, the latter being the primary means of expressing the former.

## A Place to Stand

So Baptists have learned that when we begin to worship God, He immediately calls us to love other people. Now, as long as religion is only an individual matter, one's own experience is sufficient. For, if there is a difference of opinion with others over how one ought to live, he can always say, "But this is the way I see it." And no one can contradict him. But when one obeys God's commandment to love ". . . your neighbor as yourself", he no longer stands alone before God; he now stands on equal footing with someone else whose feelings and thoughts he must respect — for Christian love is respect as much as anything. But if the experience of the other person differs from his own an impasse has been reached, for neither can claim precedence over the other. Continued relationship requires an outside authority, one which is acceptable to both. Relationships between persons are analogous to play: as long as one plays alone he can make up the rules as he plays, but if he begins to play with others the game requires an acceptance by all of a set of rules by which all will play. Otherwise, further play is impossible. Christian relationships, therefore, are basically a question of authority: what are the rules by which persons interact with one another?

The history of the Christian Church can be viewed, among other ways, as a study of the various authorities which have been followed. While Jesus lived and walked among men He was the authority for those who followed Him; those who did not accept His authority did not follow Him. But after His ascension the Church required new authority. This was lodged in Jesus' Apostles who had known Him in His earthly ministry and had witnessed His resurrection from the dead. These twelve whose names are listed in Acts 1:21-26 and, later, Paul were selected to speak in the power of the Holy Spirit in Jesus' name as the bearers of authority for the Church. But their authority was collective rather than individual as had been the case with Jesus.

Since the death of the last of these Apostles, the question of authority has been a problem. For many centuries, the Roman Catholic Church has answered this question with the claim that Jesus gave primary authority to Peter as the "Rock" upon whom the Church was built. They believe that he was the first Pope and that he has passed his authority to succeeding Popes who have, in turn, delegated it to the priesthood. Such a hierarchical location of authority has demanded a standard by which this authority could be preserved intact and made instantly available in a world in which communication was difficult and slow. Moreover, the persecutions and influences of other religions which we outlined in the previous chapter required, it was believed, some standard of distinguishing between true believers and heretics. Thus through the years a series of discussions or Councils, as they were called, were held in which the leaders of the Church debated the questions of doctrine that had arisen and decided what was true and what was false. The product of these Councils are statements called creeds which Christians must believe if they are to be members of the Church and receive her gift of salvation. These creeds as interpreted by the hierarchy of priests have become the standard of authority for the Roman Catholic

## A Place to Stand

Church. Those persons who depart from this official position are considered heretics, teachers of false doctrine. For many years heretics were hunted down, imprisoned, tortured and killed to punish their bodies in order to save their souls, as it was said.

Baptists, on the other hand, believe that apostolic authority died with the Apostles and that the authority of Jesus has been preserved in the writings about him and the writings of the Apostles which compose the Bible. These writings are the only authority for faith and morals recognized by most Baptists. But, ultimately, it is the individual's interpretation of scripture that is his final authority. Obviously, there have been many different interpretations of the same passages of scripture by different persons. It is for this reason that the Roman Catholic Church felt the necessity for a standard interpretation of scripture to be established by the hierarchy. But Baptists have usually insisted that if one is responsible for his own relationship to God, he must be free to choose without outside interference other than the Holy Spirit and scripture.

As in the case of the competency of the individual before God, there are dangers implicit in this view and, at best, there are certain conditions under which it can be fulfilled. First of all, if the Bible is to be our final authority we must know what it says. This knowledge requires that we must study it seriously and continuously. In an authoritarian system it is sufficient for the priest to know what the Bible teaches; one need only ask him what it says. But if we must make our own decisions, we must be intimate with the scriptures; otherwise our decisions are uninformed. However, we must also study it with others; for no one person is sufficient to plumb its depths alone. Different individuals see different emphases, and it is only as we share our insights that any one of us approaches a comprehensive understanding of scripture. We must read and discuss it together and so learn from each other the riches of its message. But in the final accounting, each must decide for himself what it says.

The second condition for the authority of the scripture is our obedience to it. It is not sufficient that we take what we like and ignore the rest. For scripture is a whole, and when we ignore any part of it we misinterpret all of it. When we find the Bible calling our traditions or prejudices into question, we must be prepared to abandon these in our obedience to the authority of scripture. Any other practice is to deny that authority.

A classic contemporary example of the authority of scripture over tradition and prejudice was seen in the claim of Martin Luther King, Jr. and others to Christians of all races that the Bible teaches that all followers of Jesus Christ are brothers and sisters. This claim had been ignored for centuries by many otherwise devout Christians. When they took it seriously they were compelled by the authority of scripture to submit to its witness.

There are further dangers implicit in the idea of the authority of scripture alone. One is the tendency of some to make it into an idol as the Jews treated the Law. It is easy to say that since we have the very words of God in the Bible we have all we need. It is no longer necessary to listen to God because we already have everything He has to say. This is to replace God with a book as the authority for our faith. Instead of a human Pope which the Roman Catholics have established as the foundation of their authority, such a view establishes a paper pope. This is what the Bible calls idolatry. In this case one becomes more concerned about his beliefs about the Bible than about what the Bible says.

The secular press recently reported a blatant example of this kind of bibliolatry. A seminary professor had written commentary on a particular book of the Bible for a denominational publication. Several persons criticized this commentary because, they said, it departed from Baptist teaching. The question for them was not "What does the Bible say?" The primary question for them was "Does the writer agree with what we say the Bible says?" Apparently, for such persons there is a "party line," an orthodoxy to which all denominational publications must conform. Those which do not conform must be corrected. This is creedalism in form and content.

A second danger is the tendency to devalue formal theological education. If one possesses the words of God in a book, it is said, one doesn't need to hear what anyone else has to say; God has said it all. As one such interpreter said to the author, "The Bible says what it means and means what it says." Unfortunately for such an interpretation, the Bible was written long ago and far away by persons who lived in a radically different kind of world than the world in which we live. Their thought patterns were different from ours, their manners of expression were different from ours. Indeed, the very organization of their society was different from ours. If we are to understand the Bible, we must not only read the words themselves, we must also know the political, sociological and economic context in which they were written. We must be familiar with the idiomatic expressions characteristic of the language in that locality and in that time in which it was written. In short, accurate Biblical interpretation requires a great deal more than simply what is written in the Bible. These are the subjects of Biblical scholarship which one learns in a theological seminary. This is understanding which cannot come from merely reading the Bible.

Moreover, many of the most serious contemporary problems did not exist while the Bible was being written. Problems of nuclear destruction, overpopulation, environmental pollution, abortion, birth control, human organ transplants and many others are not addressed within its pages. It provides us with general principles for living, but it often is silent on specific problems. Is one to conclude that God has nothing to say about these concerns because they are not mentioned in the Bible? As Paul often said, "God forbid!" These are the subjects of theological scholarship which one learns about through study in a seminary. This is understanding of the faith which cannot come from merely reading the Bible.

Finally, there is danger that the authority of the scripture as understood by the individual may tend to fragment the Church and her witness to the world. To allow for individual interpretation is to allow for disagreement and controversy. There have always been differences of interpretation among Baptists as

## *A Place to Stand*

well as between Baptists and other Christian groups. One recalls conflicts over slavery, missions, Christian education and many others. Indeed, the very existence of the Southern Baptist Convention itself resulted from disagreement over slavery. The revolution which we are experiencing in our Convention today is one more example of the danger of this doctrine.

Yet, after all has been said and done, we are still left with the necessity of an authority to which we can appeal when we seek to work together. Experience teaches us that the authority of scripture alone as interpreted by the individual is far less destructive than the alternatives such as creedalism and denominational authoritarianism. If we are to cooperate with one another as Jesus has commanded us to do, we must have some basis for our cooperation. We Baptists have historically voted to base our allegiance upon the authority of scripture. Like Martin Luther, we have said and continue to say, "Here I stand; I can do no other."

# 3
# We Are a Royal Priesthood

When one submits to the God of Abraham, Isaac and Jacob, the Father of Jesus and the Lord of Peter and Paul, as He has revealed Himself in the Bible, he begins a pilgrimage which does not cease this side of death. One step leads inevitably to another until all facets of one's life are affected and he is a changed person. The Bible teaches that it is not enough to trust and obey God; the Bible says that one expresses his allegiance to God by entering into loving relationships with other human beings, also. Peter put it this way: "But you are a chosen race, a royal priesthood, a holy nation, God's own people, that you may declare the wonderful deeds of him who called you out of darkness into his marvelous light." (I Peter 2:9)

One of the persistent findings of history is the fact that humans are incurably religious. Indeed, someone has defined human beings as "religious animals." Throughout our history on this earth we have been aware that something is wrong with human life. We have not always been aware of what it is or what we can do about it, but it appears almost in our bones that our lives ought to be better than they are. Out of this conviction religions have arisen in almost every human culture known to history. Man is basically a religious being; religion is his attempt to do something about what is wrong with his life.

Typically, when people have invented religions to deal with the problems of living, they have set aside certain persons called priests whose primary function has been to act as mediators between themselves and the gods, whoever they may be. It is instructive to observe that the Latin word for priest literally means "bridge builder." The priest builds bridges between the people and the gods. Most religions have felt the necessity of someone to fulfill the priestly function. It is in recognition of this fact that Peter wrote "You are . . . a royal priesthood . . ."

But we must recognize that there are distinctions between the kind of priesthood about which Peter was writing and the priesthood which most religions have established. In most other religions, priests have been persons who have been set apart from other persons because of some special talent, some special ability, some special distinction. Frequently, as was the case in ancient Israel, priests have been chosen because they belonged to certain tribes or families, and priesthood was believed to be hereditary. Because his father was a priest a certain man would be a priest; because he was a priest his son would be a priest. Or in other religions, priests were selected because of certain individual talents or experiences which set the individual apart from other human beings. A priest might be a person who had a unique sense of the mystical, who had had a particular kind of experience, who had the ability to think in abstract terms, or who simply had the patience to endure the garbage which religious people often dump upon their servants. But in almost every case priests in most religions throughout human history have been people who have been chosen out of the group because of some personal distinction.

However, this is not what Peter was talking about, nor is it what the rest of the New Testament means when it speaks of Christian priesthood. For Peter was writing to the Christian churches when he said, "But you (all) ... are a royal priesthood ..." — the personal pronoun is plural. Not some of us are priests, but all of us are priests. To be a follower of Jesus Christ, said Peter, is to be a priest.

There is a second distinction we should note between priesthood in most other religions and priesthood as Peter viewed it. The priest of a pagan religion normally interceded with his god(s) only in behalf of the followers of the religion which he served. For example, Jewish priests interceded with their God for the Jews, Roman priests interceded with their gods for Romans of their persuasion, and Greek priests for Greeks. But in the New Testament we do not find priesthood in that narrow and restricted a sense. Rather, the New Testament priest is not to intercede for the adherents of his own faith only, but also for the people of the world without concern for their religious beliefs. We are called as Christians not to be priests to our own co-religionists alone, but to minister to the whole world. That is a basic distinction between Christian priesthood and all other kinds of priesthood.

A third basic distinction of Christian priesthood concerns the function we perform. Typically, the function of the priest in most pagan religions was to make sacrifices for the people to placate the gods who were believed to be capricious if not actually hostile to the people. The priest would take whatever the people brought to him and burn it on the altar of the god with the hope that he or she would be pleased by the sacrifice of something of value. If thus pleased, the god was expected to respond by granting the petition of the worshiper.

But in the New Testament we begin with a God who loves His people. Therefore, the primary function of the priest is not to make intercession in the name of the people to God; rather, the function of the Christian priest is to bring to the people the message of God's love for them by loving them himself. Thus, the primary direction of the Christian priest's ministry is reversed from that of the priests of other religions.

It would then appear that the New Testament idea of the Priesthood of All Believers says certain important things to Baptists today. To begin, it addresses two popular contemporary views of priesthood which Baptists have usually believed are non-Biblical. The first of these views is the conception of priesthood of the Roman Catholic Church. For them, worship of God is centered around the celebration of the Lord's Supper which Catholics call the Mass. Whatever may have been the meaning of this practice in the New Testament, Catholics have developed a unique doctrine and practice for this rite. For they have decided that the Mass is a real sacrifice in the sense that the

Jews practiced sacrifice. Catholics believe that the bread becomes the real body of Jesus through the consecration of the elements by the priest. And they believe the wine becomes the actual blood of Jesus which flows again as it did almost 2000 years ago. Jesus is actually being crucified again each time the Mass is celebrated. This doctrine is symbolized in a Catholic church by the presence of the figure of Jesus on the crucifix in contrast to the empty cross seen in most Protestant churches. The absence of the figure of Jesus symbolizes the once-and-for-all-time quality of Protestant thinking about the crucifixion of Jesus.

Obviously, such sacred elements as the body and blood of Jesus, as Catholic doctrine presents, are too precious to be entrusted to ordinary ignorant, careless persons. Soameone who has been qualified by special training and granted special authority through his ordination is required to handle these elements lest they be profaned or spilled. Therefore, the function of the priesthood in the Roman Catholic Church appears to Baptists to be different from that which Peter describes.

In the second place, the Mass is viewed as being the act of dispensing the grace of God to people materially. When one eats the bread he is believed to be receiving the body of Christ materially, and the grace of God thereby. When one drinks the wine — although in usual Catholic practice the wafer is dipped into the cup and the recipient only partakes that wine which has been absorbed into the wafer — he is believed to be drinking materially the very life of Christ and receiving God's grace in that process.

Obviously, such holy elements must be administered by someone specially trained and ordained for that purpose. Thus, it appears that a crucial distinction between priesthood and laity has been established and that the church is composed primarily of the former and only in a secondary way of the latter. But the authority of the priest does not stop there. As the teacher of the congregation he holds the authority to state the accepted interpretation of the scripture and the creeds which determine membership in the Church. In a real sense the priest stands in judgment over the layperson since he determines who may receive the sacraments and who is a heretic and who is a faithful Christian.

Baptists believe this distinction between clergy and laity is non-Biblical. For the Greek words translated "clergy," which Catholics take to mean priests, and "laity," which they understand to refer to the common people, mean the same thing in the Greek language. This is one view of priesthood against which the Baptist doctrine of the Priesthood of All Believers speaks.

In the third place, the Priesthood of All Believers speaks against a view which has arisen among some Protestants in opposition to the Catholic idea of priesthood. Many who believe the New Testament clearly teaches they can approach God directly without any human mediator therefore believe they do not need any priest other than Jesus Christ Himself. But, in that case, what does Peter mean by calling us a "Royal Priesthood?" In answer to this question some say that each of us is his own priest; for them the Priesthood of All Believers speaks only

## We Are a Royal Priesthood

of the individual's relationship to himself. This also is a perversion of Peter's words; for a priest, by definition, is a mediator between two persons. Without two persons between whom reconciliation is desired, priesthood is a meaningless term.

The New Testament demonstrates that God most often approaches individuals through other individuals. He may approach one through a parent, a Sunday School teacher, a minister, or any other Christian of his acquaintance. But He initially presents Himself to the person through other human beings. This is particularly true for small children who do not have the mental capacity to deal with abstract concepts such as God or Spirit but are able to relate to concrete human beings who love and minister to their needs. This is priesthood in its basic New Testament sense, ministry by one person to another in the name of Jesus. Whereas in pagan religions the priest offers a sacrifice to the gods which someone else brings, in the Christian faith the sacrifice which the priest offers is himself. He gives his time, his interest and his energy to those to whom he ministers. As Paul said, he is a living sacrifice. But he ministers in the name of God, and he becomes the agent of God's ministry to others.

Finally, the Baptist doctrine of the Priesthood of All Believers speaks against a misunderstanding among some Baptists concerning the nature of ministry. For some have come to believe there is a distinction between the work of Christians who have been ordained and those who have not. Many readers may remember occasions when they heard preachers, particularly during revivals, call for individuals to commit themselves to "full-time Christian service." They were inviting persons to volunteer to become preachers or missionaries. But the implication of that term is that not all Christians are "full-time." Only preachers and missionaries and others in professional Church work are thought to be "full-time" Christians; the rest of us are only part-time Christians. But that is not what Peter was saying. The New Testament teaches we are all "full-time" Christians. There is no distinction in the commitment of a member of the clergy or a member of the laity. Now, our functions may be different. We may not earn our living in the same way, but we are Christians every minute of the day no matter what we do. Therefore, we are priests every minute of the day. However we may earn our living or wherever we are, we are "full-time" witnesses to our faith in Christ. This is true whether our witness is intentional or not. This is full-time Christian service. Perhaps we need to find another term to describe the distinction in function which exists between clergy and laity.

A second part of this misunderstanding is the belief of many persons that ordained ministers ought to make a greater commitment to their faith than persons who are not ordained. Perhaps we have unconsciously copied this idea from the Roman Catholic Church, which requires her priests to take three vows, poverty, chastity and obedience, which are not required of the laity. These vows bind them to renounce both ownership of material wealth and marriage and to obey their superiors in the hierarchy of the priesthood. In any case, many Baptists appear to believe that ordained persons should make a greater commitment, should live a more moral life, should sacrifice more, than other Baptists.

A young minister was called to be the pastor of a very large and wealthy Baptist church in a large Southern city. Soon after arriving on the field he was invited to the wedding reception honoring the daughter of one of the deacons of his congregation. This deacon was an influential and wealthy business man in the city, and the reception was held in the local country club. Champagne was served to the guests, and a waiter offered a glass to the minister. He took the glass and drank the champagne. The next Sunday evening the deacons of his church met in a called session and voted to ask for the minister's resignation for drinking alcoholic beverages. Apparently, it was considered acceptable for the deacons to drink champagne and to offer it to other members of the congregation. But it was not acceptable for the minister to drink it. The double standard which some have set up between clergy and laity is a denial of the New Testament teaching of the Priesthood of All Believers. If the minister should not drink alcoholic beverages, neither should any other Christian. If it is acceptable for the laity to drink them, it is also acceptable for clergy.

Finally, this double standard is seen in some views of the nature of ministry itself. A minister once called upon a layman to pray in the worship service. The latter replied, "That's what we're paying you for, preacher." In this statement, the layman revealed his misunderstanding of the doctrine of the Priesthood of All Believers. Ministry, whether it be praying or witnessing to non-Christians, is not restricted to preachers; it is the activity of all who call ourselves Christians.

The deacons of one congregation participated in a retreat recently. After it was completed, one of the deacons jokingly said, "Preacher, you've just told us we don't need you, that we can do anything you can do except perform a marriage ceremony, which is a function of the state and not of the church. If we can do anything you can do we don't need to pay you." The minister replied by saying in an equally jocular manner, "That is true; you can do anything I can do in this church. Which one of you wants to preach next Sunday?" No one responded to his question, and he is still being paid as minister of that congregation. But what was said is no less true; a Baptist church doesn't require an ordained person to lead the ministry of the people. A congregation can choose any individual and authorize him or her to perform any ministry they require.

However, a minister does offer his congregation something which is useful and unique in some respects. He offers his personality, his particular talents, and his education, which are different from others. In that sense, he can do for his church something which they cannot do for themselves. But there is no essential difference between the minister as an ordained person and any other member of a Baptist congregation. We are all evangelists, we are all missionaries, we are all witnesses, we are all teachers; in short, we are all priests in every sense of the word. Thus, it is to each of us that Peter was writing when he wrote that our purpose as followers of Jesus Christ is to "... declare the wonderful deeds of him who called you out of darkness into his marvelous light." We are priests to one another; we are priests to the world.

# 4
# An Essential Difference

We have been discussing what it means to be a Baptist. Thus far, we have identified three doctrines which we have shared with most other Protestants. But now we are going to part company with them because we are taking up a doctrine in which Baptists disagree with most Protestants, the doctrine of a Regenerate Church. For Baptists have usually believed that in order for an individual to become a member of Christ's body, the Church, he must make his own decision; it cannot be made for him by someone else. The following scripture is an example of the Biblical evidence upon which Baptists have founded this doctrine.

> Now when they heard this they were cut to the heart, and said to Peter and to the rest of the apostles, "Brethren, what shall we do?" And Peter said to them, "Repent, and be baptized every one of you in the name of Jesus Christ for the forgiveness of your sins; and you shall receive the gift of the Holy Spirit. For the promise is to you and to your children and to all that are far off, every one whom the Lord our God calls to him." And he testified with many other words and exhorted them, saying, "Save yourselves from this crooked generation." So those who received his word were baptized, and there were added that day about three

thousand souls. And they devoted themselves to the apostles' teaching and fellowship, to the breaking of bread and the prayers. (Acts 2:37-42)

It was at Pentecost that the Christian Church came into being. Jesus had collected a group of disciples who followed Him while He lived upon the earth. After His resurrection He had instructed them to wait in Jerusalem for the coming of the Holy Spirit, which Acts tells us occurred at Pentecost. Something happened on that occasion which changed those followers of Jesus into the Church. Those who witnessed this event were struck by its uniqueness. They didn't understand what was happening, but they could not ignore it. So they asked the participants what was ging on. Acts reports that Peter responded by preaching a sermon. In this sermon he made three assertions. He stated that (1) Jesus of Nazareth was the fulfillment of the Old Testament prophecies that God would send a Messiah to save His people from their oppressors; (2) when Jesus came Israel had rejected Him and had had Him killed; and (3) God had raised Him from the dead and had, thereby, proved that He is Lord over death as well as life.

Some of the people who had heard Peter's sermon were "... cut to the heart." They were convinced that somehow they had been involved in the execution of Jesus, which was a great offense to God. So they cried to Peter, "What shall we do?" He replied that, first of all, they must repent their alienation from God; secondly, they must be baptized, and finally, they would receive the gift of the Holy Spirit into their lives.

## An Essential Difference

The primary thrust of this account is the report that a number of persons became convinced, individually, that their relationships with the God of creation were not satisfactory and that it was necessary for them to enter into new relationships with Him so that they could know life as it is intended to be. It appears obvious that the three thousand persons who joined the Church on Pentecost did so because each had decided for himself that he needed to change his own personal relationship with the God of Israel. Therefore, each as a result of his own decision was baptized and received into the Church.

This event, Baptists believe, is characteristic of the process by which the Church came into being and spread over the New Testament world. A key issue here is that each person made his own decision both to change his relationship with God and, then, to join the Church. Neither decision was made for anyone by another. A second key issue concerns the order of decisions and events. The decision to change one's relationship with God always preceded the decision to unite with the Church. One was baptized only after receiving the gift of salvation, for Baptism is a symbol of what has already happened. It is one's profession of faith in the God of Jesus Christ to free him from slavery to sin and death; it is a symbolic identification with the death, burial and resurrection of Jesus; it is a symbol of the washing of the stain of sin from one's self; and it is the symbol of new birth which Jesus mentioned to Nicodemus.

Most New Testament scholars today admit that Baptism was always by immersion in the New Testament accounts. Indeed, the meaning of the Greek word from which we derive the English word *baptize* literally means "immerse" or "dip." This is the way Baptists read the New Testament.

But Church history records that with the passage of time changes began to be made in the sequence of events involving joining the Church. While the change from a symbolic interpretation of the Lord's Supper into a sacramental interpretation was occurring, changes were also taking place in the thinking of the nature of the Church and of Baptism. Just as the Supper came to be seen as the means by which the grace of God is dispensed to persons materially, so also Baptism came to be understood as the necessary and sufficient act through which one is saved from sin and death. Of course, if that interpretation is true, if it is necessary for a person to be baptized to be saved from hell, then it becomes very important to baptize all persons as quickly after birth as possible. This was particularly true in the ancient world and during the Dark Ages when many children died in the first year after birth. Thus, one must see that his child is baptized immediately after being born if one wishes to insure the child will go to heaven to live with Christ. Indeed, the Roman Catholic Church eventually went so far as to develop a practice called "interuterine Baptism" in which, if it should become apparent that the mother will die before delivery or that the child will be stillborn, Baptism may be performed on the fetus in the womb before birth occurs. If a child should die before Baptist can be administered, Roman Catholic doctrine teaches that he will go to a place called "Limbo," a part of hell reserved

## An Essential Difference

particularly for such persons. This is the result of the belief that salvation and grace are given to the person through the administration of the sacraments. Without the sacraments, it is believed, there can be no salvation.

The Reformers of the sixteenth century, Luther, Calvin, Zwingli, and others, recognized the difference between the teaching of the New Testament and the practice of the Roman Catholic Church of their day. They had discovered that the individual must accept for himself this grace that God offers us; it cannot be conferred upon him by anyone else, not by the Church, not by parents nor by teachers. They had begun to see, as the New Testament had taught, the necessity for each individual to make his own decision with regard to his relationships to God and the Church. But then they were caught in a dilemma.

All of the churches in the period of the Reformation of the sixteenth century were state churches, that is to say that the churches were a part of the governments of the principalities in which they resided. The states supported the churches with money raised from taxes. The states also protected the churches from the threat of heresy as well as the threat of persecution by the Catholic church. Indeed, in many cases the states ruled the churches within their realms through the appointment of bishops and other church officials. There was a doctrine which said, "Whose rule, his church." When Martin Luther led his followers to establish a new church following their excommunication by the Pope, they were protected from repression from armies under Cathlic princes because Luther's ruler, Prince Frederick of

Saxony, agreed with Luther. In a similar manner, John Calvin and his followers were protected from Catholic persecution because Calvin had been able to persuade the city fathers of Geneva that his way of interpreting scripture was right and that of the Roman Catholic Church was wrong. Therefore, the Geneva fathers passed a law that henceforth Geneva would be Calvinist.

Herein lies the dilemma which faced the Reformers: Baptism was a political act as well as a religious act; it not only conferred church membership upon the recipient, it also conferred citizenship in the state. Indeed, for centuries the only birth records in many countries were the baptismal records of the various churches. To be a citizen of Saxony was also to be a Lutheran; to be a citizen of Geneva was also to be a Calvinist. As long as the Protestant churches were a part of the state, they were under the protection of that state from outside interference from other Protestants as well as from Catholics.

Such were the political currents of the time that Luther, Calvin and others were afraid to renounce this connection with the state for fear of what might happen if they did not continue to enjoy the protection of the states. Subsequent history amply demonstrates that it was only such protection by the secular power of the states which enabled the reformed churches to continue to exist. Some forerunners of modern Baptists were wiped out because they did not have state protection. But in order to retain this protection, infant Baptism was also retained by most of the new Protestant churches although their new-found Biblical understanding undermined its theological foundations.

## An Essential Difference

Therefore, it became necessary for the Reformers to find justification for what they were already doing. They read in Matthew 19:13-15 that Jesus said, "Let the children come to me, and do not hinder them; for to such belongs the kingdom of heaven." They interpreted this to mean that Jesus invited infants to be baptized into church membership. Acts 16:15 reports that Lydia of Philippi was baptized ". . . with her household, . . ." and it was assumed this included infants. The same chapter also states that the Philippian jailor was baptized ". . . with all his family," which also was assumed to include infants. This was accepted as Biblical basis for infant Baptism.

Others turned to the Old Testament and concluded that just as circumcision was the sign and seal of God's covenant with Abraham and his descendants, so Baptism is the sign and seal of God's covenant with His Church. Therefore, just as circumcision was administered to the new-born Jew, so also Baptism should be administered to the new-born Christian.

But the conflict between a doctrine which maintained that each individual person must make his own submission to God and a political practice of having the Church make this decision for the individual continued to provoke dissatisfaction in many quarters. Some Lutherans sought to solve the problem by saying that Baptism confers faith as well as salvation upon the recipient. Others said that the baptism of an infant is the symbol of the fact that God does everything in salvation and the individual contributes nothing.

Eventually, however, these churches were forced by their Biblical understanding to invent the idea of confirmation; at some time during the life of the recipient when he becomes aware of what he is doing and becomes responsible for his decisions he must confirm his baptism for himself. He may have been baptized as an infant, but at some time — usually around the age of twelve — he is expected to make his own decision to be a disciple of Jesus Christ. This is essentially what Baptists have believed all along.

Later, John Wesley was driven by the force of events to invent the concept of "backsliding." For he saw in England all of those millions of persons who had been baptized in infancy into the Church of England but who never showed any sign, either in their manner of living or in church participation, that they were Christians. Indeed, it has been estimated that in the time of Wesley scarcely more than ten percent of the people of England, virtually all of whom had been baptized as infants, participated in the life of the Church of England at all. So Wesley raised the question of why so many people who are in the Church do not act like it. Instead of questioning the practice of infant Baptism and the nature of Church membership, he invented the concept of "backsliding," which teaches that one can be brought into the Church through infant Baptism and, then, through inattention to the sacraments or through some mortal sin, he can "backslide" out of the Church.

Baptists, however, are convinced the New Testament teaches that a person cannot be brought into the Church unless he decides to become a member. We believe the decision to join the Church is an individual choice and that only those persons who have made it for themselves can enter the Church, Baptism or no Baptism. Therefore, we believe the New

## An Essential Difference

Testament requires the Church to be regenerate; that is, composed only of persons who have been reborn in Christ. Only after receiving salvation can one request church membership and be baptized into the Body of Christ. Although we have usually insisted that the symbolic value of the ordinance is conveyed only by immersion, the mode has always been secondary to the primary requirement that the individual has made his own decision to follow Christ.

In this belief, Baptists have parted company with most other Protestants, for most Protestants still practice infant Baptism although the political basis for it has long since passed in the United States and many European countries. But let us not become smug in thinking that we are right and others are wrong. Let us not believe we are superior to Protestants who continue to practice infant Baptism. Although we believe our doctrine is, in fact, closer to the teaching of the New Testament, our practice has not always kept pace with our doctrine.

In our emphasis upon the importance of the initial decision, Baptists have sometimes over-emphasized that decision; we have resorted to a practice which one minister called "dip 'um and drap 'um." We have convinced persons to make a decision for Christ, we have baptized them, and then we have often forgotten all about them in our continued quest for new converts. In our emphasis upon church growth and mass evangelism, we have often persuaded many persons to make decisions and to be baptized into church membership as if that is all that is required for salvation. We have sometimes forgotten that Jesus spoke of life in the Kingdom of God as a process beginning with a new birth and continuing as one grows toward Christian maturity. Likewise, we have sometimes forgotten Paul's instruction to the Philippian Christians to work out their own salvation with fear and trembling.

Moreover, some Baptists, on occasion, have come close to the practice of infant Baptism by immersing children of three and four years of age. Can it be seriously maintained that a three-year-old has significantly more understanding of the nature of God or of his own relationship to Him than an infant? Many of us have been so concerned to evangelize the world in our time and to enlarge our church statistics that we have approached, if we have not actually succeeded in, perverting our own doctrines of Believer's Baptism and a Regenerate Church.

Sometimes one wonders if Baptism makes any difference at all. For when we compare Baptists who believe and practice Believer's Baptism by immersion with other Protestants who do not so believe or practice, it is difficult to discover any appreciable differences in our manners of living or witness to Christ. One sometimes wonders if it makes any difference at what age persons are baptized or if they are baptized at all. A study of the rolls of most churches and the numbers of persons who have no apparent allegiance to Christ or to His Church which baptized them suggests that in many cases the ages of those persons when they received Baptism matter little. We have received millions of persons into our churches who not only never attend or support those churches, they no longer even live in the communities where their church membership resides. We Southern Bap-

## An Essential Difference

tists claim some fourteen million church members; of those, a full four million are non-resident. In what sense can they be considered members — "parts of the body" in Paul's use of the term? Is "backsliding" the cause of such disinterest, as John Wesley suggested? Lest we become snug and feel superior because we are closer to the New Testament than others, let us remember that our doctrine may be superior to our practice.

But after all else is said and done, to be a Baptist is to believe among other things that the Church of Jesus Christ is composed only of those persons who have repented of their alienation from God, who have entered into a new relationship of trust with Him in Christ, and who, only then, have entered the Church through Baptism by immersion. This is an essential difference between Baptists and most other Christian groups.

# 5
# On Getting Down to Brass Tacks

A recent article in the secular press contained a statement which was puzzling to many Baptists. The pastor of a church which calls itself Baptist boldly proclaimed that he is an authoritarian leader. He said most decisions in his church are made by him and three or four lay leaders. If that minister had been a Roman Catholic priest or even a Methodist minister, one might not have been surprised at this statement because those churches give to the local minister great authority within his congregation. But Baptist history amply demonstrates that decisions in most Baptist churches are made by majority vote of the congregation, not by the minister and a few lay leaders.

The identification of this minister with the group which has taken control of the Southern Baptist Convention in recent years makes one wonder if these people who call themselves Baptists really know what Baptists have historically believed. For when we get down to brass tacks, Baptists have usually concerned ourselves most vigorously with religious liberty above all other considerations.

Because we have normally sought authority for our beliefs and practices from the Bible, Baptists have searched there for guidance in structuring our churches. But when one reads the New Testament to discover how churches were organized in the first century, he soon encounters a problem. There was apparently more than one pattern by which the early churches were organized. Indeed, there appear to have been at least three distinct patterns. The sixth chapter of Acts describes the selection of those servants who were to administer to the widows of the Hellenists — we call these servants deacons today — as if it were done by the congregation as a whole. On the other hand, Acts 14:23 states that Paul and Barnabas appointed elders to preside over the church which they had established in Galatia. Finally, I Timothy and III John give the impression that bishops were already common among the churches. It may be that this evidence is too scanty to bear such a burden, but it does appear that churches were structured according to various patterns during the first century.

So, it is difficult to find in the New Testament any one authoritative pattern by which churches were structured. We Baptists have concluded, however, that the only way to organize a congregation is upon the basis of those same distinctives which have motivated us to identify ourselves in contrast to other Christian groups. As we have stated before, Baptists began with the conviction that every person must decide for himself what his relationship with God will be. That idea is fundamental. The second distinctive is the belief that the only authority we have is the Bible; we must be able to justify everything we believe and do upon the basis of what the Bible says. The third distinctive we claim is the belief that every Christian is a priest, not to himself, but to others. Each of us is a minister; there is no distinction between clergy and laity. Therefore, no one has any more authority than anyone else because we all stand equal before God as sinners and as redeemed persons. Finally, Baptists have usually believed that the only persons who can join the Church are persons who have chosen to do so by their own decision; we do not baptize infants because we do not believe they can make that kind of decision for themselves.

When one takes these distinctives and seeks to integrate them into one church organization, he arrives by necessity at a pure democracy. All authority within the Church resides in the congregation as a whole. There is no one person, be he pastor or deacon, who possesses the authority to tell another church member what he must believe or do. Authority resides in the congregation, and all decisions must be made by majority vote of that body. Upon this basis certain individuals and groups may be authorized by the congregation to fulfill specific functions, but the congregation always stands in oversight of the fulfillment of these functions and always reserves the authority to recall any who fail to discharge their delegated responsibilities at any time. A Baptist church is by its very nature a pure democracy.

Perhaps, if all Baptist congregations had remained isolated from all other Baptist congregations, we could have avoided the problems which face our Convention today. But it soon became apparent to many of our forefathers that individual congregations did not possess the resources necessary to carry on many of the ministries which were needed in the world. To begin, in the early periods of Baptist life in this country most Baptist churches were very small. In addition, the Baptists of that time drew most of their constituents from the more humble classes of people; not many wealthy nor many highly educated persons were attracted to the Baptist point of view in those days. As is usually the case, established religion undergirds privilege, and the privileged people of a society are not usually drawn to dissenting religious groups.

Therefore, it was perceived to be nearly impossible for a single Baptist congregation to send a missionary half-way around the world and to maintain him there. In a similar manner, it was seen to be very difficult for a single church to establish a college and to maintain it for the instruction of preachers, teachers and missionaries. Moreover, social services such as hospitals, orphanages and homes for the aging were beyond the means of most early Baptist churches. Some of our forebears saw that in order to provide those ministries which they believed were the necessary work of the churches, individual Baptist congregations must band together, pool their resources, and cooperate for the accomplishment of ministries which they could not accomplish separately.

In order to realize this dream of world-wide missionary, educational and social service ministries, our forefathers began to form organizations: first, associations which were local in geography; then, conventions which linked the efforts of churches within a state; finally, conventions which sought to enlist churches throughout the whole country as it then existed. The key issue in these efforts at cooperation was the insistence by all that the individual church retained its autonomy unabridged and that the cooperation was purely voluntary. This independence was to be assured through the composition of the larger bodies and their relationships to one another and to the churches. Associations and conventions were composed not of churches but of individual messengers who had been elected by the churches. Each congregation, association and convention was completely independent of all others in its own sphere. Therefore, congregations were not to instruct their messengers to associations and conventions as to their voting. Likewise, associations and conventions were not to bind churches by their decisions, nor were they to concern themselves with specifically congregational matters such as church membership and leadership. The one absolutely forbidden element in such denominational cooperation has been a doctrinal test of faith or creed. Belief is an individual matter, not a denominational concern. Indeed, the very organization of the Southern Baptist Convention in 1845 resulted from opposition to a doctrinal test of faith by a missionary agency.

The earliest support for missions among Baptists in America came from independently organized mission societies in the late nineteenth century. These societies consisted only of the individuals who constituted them from year to year, but agents such as Luther Rice were employed to contact the various churches on the Atlantic seaboard for the purpose of raising money for the support of foreign and home missionaries. This method proved to be moderately successful until the issue of slavery was made a test of faith for all persons who applied for appointment by the mission societies. In 1844, the ownership of slaves was made a disqualification for appointment by the Home Mission Society. Since much support for missions had previously come from slave holders in the South, and since a number of missionaries who had already been appointed were slaveholders, many Southern proponents of missions felt they had been discriminated against by this policy.

Therefore, on May 8, 1845, a total of 327 messengers from eleven states met in Augusta, Georgia, and organized the Southern Baptist Convention. Not all of those messengers were slaveholders, nor were all of them supporters of slavery. But they felt that Baptists should not discriminate against one another on the basis of doctrinal differences in the administration of their missionary efforts. In this light it was a primary concern of the founders of this Convention that doctrinal matters not become a test of faith for persons who might engage in the work of the Convention.

Cooperation without regard to belief was a fundamental concern of the framers of the Southern Baptist Convention, but in recent years we have seen this concern being eroded by certain parties. These individuals have banded together in a blatant effort to seize control of the Convention. They have already gained control of the presidency of the Convention for several years. Now they are seeking to gain

## On Getting Down to Brass Tacks

control of the boards of trustees of the agencies through which the Convention does its work. The President of the Convention nominates the Nominating Committee which, in turn, nominates the Committee on Boards. This latter committee then nominates candidates for election by the Convention to the various boards of trustees of the agencies. By packing the Nominating Committee with persons of his particular point of view, the President is able to assure that trustees are also compatible with his convictions. In the past several years nominees for these boards have usually been those who assent to a doctrinal test of faith: the inerrancy of the original manuscripts of the various books of the Bible.

It is not the purpose of this discussion to debate the truth or falsity of this assertion. On the contrary, the purpose of this essay is to show that the attempt to make a doctrinal test of faith for participation in work of the Southern Baptist Convention is a radical departure from Baptist thought and practice throughout our history. For Baptists have always believed that no one can dictate to another what he must believe; associations and conventions have never been formed upon the basis of creeds. As has been stated above, the historical basis for denominational cooperation has been solely the purpose of pooling resources to conduct missions and other ministries which individual congregations could not accomplish alone. Thus, any convention which takes upon itself the authority to establish what Baptists must believe has ceased at that point to be Baptistic in any historical sense of the word and has become, instead, a creedal body. When such a step is taken the road is open to an authoritarianism such as the Roman Catholics practice. That is a repudiation of the fundamental issue upon which Baptists originated and upon which we have stood throughout our history.

Thus, the current trend in the Southern Baptist Convention to make it a creedal body is a serious threat to the continued existence of that body. Baptists have always been concerned about religious liberty because we were born in persecution. In many of the colonies prior to the American revolution, it was illegal for Baptists to hold worship services. Every citizen of those colonies was automatically baptized into the Church of England or into one of the other established churches, and every citizen was required to pay taxes to support that established church. Anyone who sought to worship in any other form or believe any other doctrine was, thereby, breaking the law. It was against the law for Baptists to meet in those colonies, and many Baptist meeting houses were locked by the authorities. It was against the law for a Baptist preacher to preach in those same colonies and many Baptist preachers were thrown into jail. This is the reason many of our forefathers supported the American revolution against England. This is the reason they were concerned that the First Amendment to the Constitution of the United States be adopted to insure religious liberty for all.

It now appears that religious liberty is being threatened not by the state or by an established church but by members of our own Convention. Historically, religious liberty has been a prime concern if not *the* prime concern of most Baptists. We have been convinced that in order to guarantee our own freedom of conscience we must be willing to guarantee the freedom of conscience of all others, for a threat to the religious liberty of any is a threat to the liberty of all. Baptists have cooperated for missions and other ministries only with the assurance that our liberties are guaranteed by all groups and individuals with whom we have cooperated. For some to seek to establish a test of faith for participation in those ministries — even were we to agree with the doctrine or idea proposed — is to threaten the very basis of Christian fellowship and cooperation itself. Such an attempt is a threat to our very being because it seeks to usurp the most important decision of our lives. It is a threat to which Baptists cannot surrender and continue to live in any meaningful way.

# 6
# Conclusions

As we have maintained throughout this discussion, Baptists are in general agreement with most other Protestant Christian groups as to the essentials of the Gospel of Jesus Christ proclaimed in the Bible. We have differed with others primarily in the implementation of that Gospel in our daily lives. Therefore, it is vital to understand that Baptist distinctives concern themselves not with the essence of the Gospel but with its organization and practice. This relationship between the essence and practice may be compared to that which exists between the constitution of an organization and its by-laws. The constitution sets forth the purpose and general principles of the organization while the by-laws state the methods by which the former will be realized. Many organizations are established for the accomplishment of similar purposes, but each may be organized and operated differently. Baptist distinctives are our method for carrying out what we believe are the imperatives of our faith. Therefore, while not of ultimate importance in themselves, they are nonetheless vital to our understanding of who we are and to our witness to others.

This discussion has sought to set forth these distinctives which called the Southern Baptist Convention into existence and which have determined the methods by which it has operated for one hundred forty years. The history of Southern Baptists strongly suggests that the primary purpose of the organizers of this Convention in 1845 was to facilitate the cooperation of churches for missions and other ministries which could not be accomplished by single congregations alone. Because this Convention was born as the result of doctrinal dispute, her framers were determined to eliminate doctrinal conflicts from its operations. For it was the 1844 decision of the American Baptist Home Mission Society in Boston to deny missionary appointment to slave-holders which precipitated organization of the Southern Baptist Convention. Therefore, the requirement for participation in her deliberations has been the contribution of money to her causes.

Recently, however, there has appeared a new or different breed of persons calling themselves Southern Baptists who wish to rewrite history and to change the rules of the game by which Baptists cooperate. These persons insist, all evidence to the contrary notwithstanding, that historically a Baptist has been a person who believed in the inerrancy of the original manuscripts of the books of the Bible. They further insist that persons who do not believe in this inerrancy are not, by definition, Baptists. For these neo-Baptists — as we shall call them — cooperation must be founded on orthodoxy with respect to their view of the Bible. Without this common bond of doctrine — creed, some might call it — there can be no fellowship or cooperation for anything. We who disagree with them are heretics who must be eliminated by whatever method needed to maintain the purity of the body-politic.

As one reads of this controversy, he is reminded of the controversies in the first three centuries of church history. As was the case then, so now the struggles and uncertainties of the surrounding political, economic and social climate appear in the minds of many to threaten the continued existence of the Church. "Atheistic humanism," "godless communism" and liberalism are perceived to be undermining the structure of the Church and the proclamation of the Gospel even as Gnosticism and the mystery religions of the early Christian era appeared to undermine the orthodoxy of the Church at that time. Government interference in the free expression of religion in community and public school functions suggest to many of persecution similar to that experienced by the Church under the Roman Empire. Religious toleration of differing religious beliefs and practices is believed to lead directly into heresies which dilute the purity of the Gospel and sap the vitality of evangelistic and missionary zeal. In a manner similar to that of the early Church, which felt the necessity to withdraw into the apparent security of creedal and hierarchical authoritarianism, many contemporary members of Baptist churches are being tempted by the rapid changes and political, economic and social struggles of modern technological society to do the same. The major difference between this thinking in the third century and in the current century is the greater rapidity with which the neo-Baptists are moving today.

This is a revolution among Southern Baptists. For the Baptist Distinctives by which we have been living for several centuries do not allow a creed or doctrinal test of faith. Indeed, they are the very antithesis of such. What is at stake, then, is the very meaning of the concept of Baptist.

While this is the basic question at issue in the current controversy among us, other issues are also involved. The neo-Baptists are very careful to stipulate that inerrancy applies only to the autographs of the various writings which compose the Bible. But not even the most ardent proponent of this view claims the existence of one of these autographs. If this be true, what sense does it make to build an argument upon evidence which is not available? If they admit, as most of them do, that they do not possess an inerrant version of the Bible, what difference does it make if the originals were inerrant or not? This is hardly a sufficient issue upon which to destroy the Convention and her world-wide ministries.

A second question is related to the first. Because most contemporary Southern Baptists normally read from a version of the Bible which has been translated from the original Hebrew, Aramaic and Greek languages, what has happened to the inerrancy claimed for the writings in the original languages? Unless the translators were also preserved from error by the Holy Spirit, has not inerrancy been lost in translation? And if this is the case, of what use is inerrancy to the millions of Baptists who cannot read the Bible in the original languages?

## Conclusions

Finally, the question of authority must be raised again. If the neo-Baptists claim the Bible as their final authority, as most of them do, where do they find the Biblical basis for their claim of inerrancy for the autographs of the Biblical writings? After some thirty years of intensive study, the present writer has yet to discover within its pages a statement which even remotely suggests that the Bible claims inerrancy for itself. Indeed, a careful reading of Paul's letters will demonstrate his humility about his own ideas in contrast with the teaching of the Holy Spirit (I Corinthians 7:25ff., for instance). The Gospel of John speaks only of Jesus as the "Word of God." So what is their authority for making such a claim for the Bible which it does not claim for itself. And what is their authority for creating such divisions among their supposed brothers and sisters in Jesus Christ as their claim is provoking? Surely there is some other basis for their claims, but until the present time they have not revealed it. In the meantime, those of us who operate on the foundation of the aforesaid Baptist Distinctives must continue to do so as we have done for one hundred forty years.

But even without an understandably rational basis for this attack, the neo-Baptists represent a serious threat to the continuation of Southern Baptist mission activity in the world. For if they succeed in disqualifying all of us who disagree with them as to what a Baptist is, they will eliminate a majority of those Baptists who have been supporting Southern Baptist Convention missions and ministries through the years. If we are not allowed to continue to participate in the decision-making process of Southern Baptist mission activities, why should we continue to support it? While there may not be a dramatic division in which a large number of messengers will walk out of a Convention as has sometimes occurred at political conventions, there may very well be a gradual falling away of the support of churches as they transfer their financial support to other organizations which seek to accomplish similar purposes. This may well occur when the neo-Baptists have acquired a majority of the trustees of the various Convention agencies and when seminary professors and other agency employees are being attacked and removed for doctrinal reasons. One may reasonably expect that as such events occur, financial support for Convention causes will diminish rapidly because neo-Baptists have never demonstrated much interest in cooperative financial ventures over a long period of time. Rather, they have tended to divide and splinter whatever groups they have entered after a short period of time, just as they are doing in our Convention today. It appears probable that the ultimate result of this revolution will be the radical diminution or even the total dissolution of the ministries which have arisen out of the Southern Baptist Convention. Even the demise of the Convention itself does not appear to be beyond the realm of possibility.

Southern Baptists have reached a vital crossroads in our community existence. The decisions we make in the next few years will likely have far-reaching consequences upon our future as a Convention and a denomination. Let us study our past carefully as we make these decisions.

# Partial Bibliography
# and Suggested Reading

Bainton, Roland H. *The Reformation of the Sixteenth Century.* Boston: The Beacon Press, 1952.

Barnes, W. W. *The Southern Baptist Convention 1845-1953.* Nashville: Broadman Press, 1954.

Barth, Karl. *The Teaching of the Church Regarding Baptism.* Translated by Ernest A. Payne. London: SCM Press, 1961.

Brown, Robert McAfee. *The Spirit of Protestantism.* New York: Oxford University Press, 1961.

Brunner, Emil. *Dogmatics: Volume 3. The Christian Doctrine of the Church, Faith, and the Consummation.* Translated by David Cairns and T. H. L. Parker. Philadelphia: The Westminster Press, 1962.

_____. *The Misunderstanding of the Church.* Translated by Harold Knight. Philadelphia: The Westminster Press, 1953.

Carr, Warren. *Baptism: Conscience and Clue for the Church.* New York: Holt, Rinehart and Winston, 1964.

Hays, Brooks, & Steely, John E. *The Baptist Way of Life,* rev. ed. Macon, Georgia: Mercer University Press, 1981.

Howe, Claude L., Jr., ed. *Glimpses of Baptist Heritage.* Nashville: Broadman Press, 1981.

Kung, Hans. *The Church.* Garden City, New York: Image Books, 1976.

McCall, Duke K., ed. *What is the Church?* Nashville: Broadman Press, 1958.

McNutt, William Roy. *Polity and Practice in Baptist Churches.* Philadelphia: Judson Press, 1935.

Robinson, H. Wheeler. *The Life and Faith of the Baptists.* Wake Forest, North Carolina: Stevens Book Press, 1985.

Shurden, Walter B., ed. *The Life of the Baptists in the Life of the World.* Nashville: Broadman Press, 1985.

Stealey, Sydnor L., ed. *A Baptist Treasury.* New York: Thomas Y. Crowell Co., 1958.

Sullivan, James L. *Baptist Polity as I See It*. Nashville: Broadman Press, 1983.

Torbet, Robert G. *A History of the Baptists*. Philadelphia: Judson Press, 1950.

Walker, Williston et al. *A History of the Christian Church*, 4th ed. New York: Charles Scribner's Sons, 1985.